And again for my parents

small poems again

by Valerie Worth
pictures by Natalie Babbitt

Farrar, Straus and Giroux   *New York*

Poems copyright © 1975, 1986 by Valerie Worth
Pictures copyright © 1986 by Natalie Babbitt
All rights reserved
Library of Congress catalog card number: 85-47513
Published simultaneously in Canada by
Collins Publishers, Toronto
Printed in the United States of America
First edition, 1986
Second printing, 1988

small poems again

amoeba

Never wondering
What shape to take,
But with a
Slow shrug
Making a start
In any direction,
And then following,
Flowing wholeheartedly
Into the fluid
Mold of the moment.

jacks

The way
Jacks nest
Together in
The hand,

Or cupped
Between
Two palms,
Jingled up

And thrown,
Land in a
Loose starry
Cluster,

Seems luxury
Enough,
Without the
Further bliss

Of their
Slender
Iridescent
Luster.

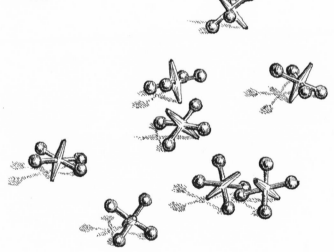

anteater

Imagine overturning
The teeming anthill
Without a qualm,
Calmly sweeping
Up its angry
Inhabitants on a
Long sticky tongue,
And swallowing the
Lot with relish—
As if those
Beady little bodies
Made just so many
Mouthfuls of red
Or black caviar.

frost

How does
The plain
Transparency
Of water

Sprout these
Lacy fronds
And plumes
And tendrils?

And where,
Before window-
Panes, did
They root

Their lush
Crystal forests,
Their cold
Silver jungles?

beetle

As in old
Mummy-times,
The scarab
Beetle keeps
Its precious
Innards
Packed in
A lacquered
Coffer of
Curious
Compartments.

robins

Look how
Last year's
Leaves, faded
So gray
And brown,

Blunder
Along
Like flimsy
Flightless
Birds,

Stumbling
Beak over
Tail
Before
The wind.

But no,
Wait:
Today
They right
Themselves,

And turn
To the
Stout slate
And ruddy
Rust

Of robins,
Running
On steady
Stems across
The ground.

kaleidoscope

Only a litter
Of bright bits,
Tipped and tumbled
Over each other
Until they huddle
Untidily all
In one corner,

Where their
Reflections wake
And break into
Crystals, petals,
Stars: only
The tricks of
Mirrors, but

Still miracles,
Like snowflakes
Shaken from jumbled
Clouds, or earth's
Rough muddle
Jostled to
Jewels and flowers.

tiger

The tiger
Has swallowed
A black sun,

In his cold
Cage he
Carries it still:

Black flames
Flicker through
His fur,

Black rays roar
From the centers
Of his eyes.

mantis

Bowing
Such lean
And monklike
Shoulders,

Robed in
Such leafily
Meek
Array,

Folding
The wrists,
And treading
So slowly,

Can it
Really be
Wholly
Holy,

Pretending
To pray,
While intending
To prey?

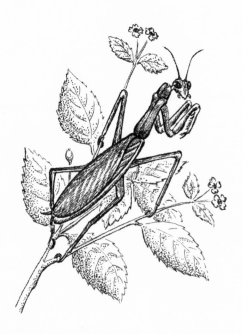

seashell

My father's mother
Picked up the shell
And turned it about
In her hand that was
Crinkled, glossy and
Twined with veins,
The fingers rumpled
Into soft roses
At the knuckles, and
She said, "Why did
That little creature
Take so much trouble
To be beautiful?"

asparagus

Like a nest
Of snakes
Awakened, craning
Long-necked

Out of the
Ground: to stand
With sharp
Scaly heads

Alert, tasting
The air,
Taking the sun,
Looking around.

telephone poles

Close by,
They're stolid
Stumps, sweating
Black creosote,
Scarred with
Bolts and tin
Numbers, clumsy
Old dolts
Of lumber;

But wandering
Away, they
Lean into
The cloud's
Drift, the
Swallow's slant,
The graceful
Influence of
Grass; and

Lifting up
Their long
Electric lines,
They hand
Them on
And on, in
Gestures of
Exquisite
Gossamer.

starfish

Spined
With sparks,
Limbed
With flames,

Climbing
The dark
To cling
And shine

Until the
Slow tide
Turns
Again:

Not even
Knowing
What stars
Are,

But
Even so,
The
Same.

crows

When the high
Snows lie worn
To rags along
The muddy furrows,

And the frozen
Sky frays, drooping
Gray and sodden
To the ground,

The sleek crows
Appear, flying
Low across the
Threadbare meadow

To jeer at
Winter's ruin
With their jubilant
Thaw, thaw, thaw!

fleas

Roaming these
Furry prairies,
Daring every so
Often to stop
And sink a well
In the soft pink
Soil, hoping
To draw up a
Hasty drop, and
Drink, and survive,

There's always
The threat of those
Inexplicable storms,
When over the hairy
Horizon rages
A terrible paw:
Descending to
Rend the ground,
While we scramble
Away for our lives.

coat hangers

Open the closet
And there they
Wait, in a
Trim obedient row;

Stirred by the
Air, they only
Touch wires with
A vacant jangle;

But try to
Remove just one,
And they suddenly
Clash and cling,

And fling them-
Selves to the
Floor in an
Inextricable tangle.

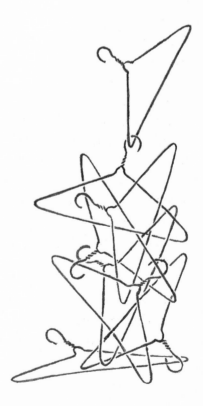

dandelion

Out of
Green space,
A sun:
Bright for
A day, burning
Away to
A husk, a
Cratered moon:

Burst
In a week
To dust:
Seeding
The infinite
Lawn with
Its starry
Smithereens.

heron

Only
Fools
Pursue
Their
Prey.

Mine
Comes to
Me, while
I stand and
Reflect:

Quick silver
Visions
Swimming into
My glassy
Reverie,

Seized
By a mere
Nod of
My wise
Beak.

library

No need even
To take out
A book: only
Go inside
And savor
The heady
Dry breath of
Ink and paper,
Or stand and
Listen to the
Silent twitter
Of a billion
Tiny busy
Black words.

octopus

Marvel at the
Awful many-armed
Sea-god Octopus,
And the coiled
Elbows of his eager
Eightfold embrace;

Yet also at his
Tapered tender
Fingertips, ferrying
Their great brow
Along the sea floor
In solitary grace.

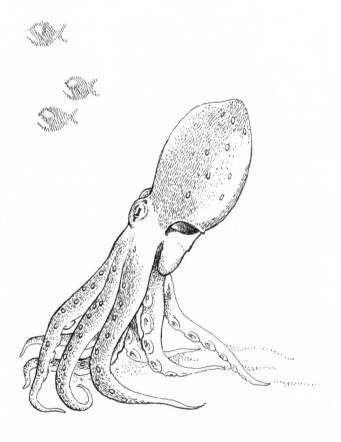

skunk

Sometimes, around
Moonrise, a wraith
Drifts in through
The open window:
A vague cold taint
Of rank weeds
And phosphorescent ·
Mold, a hint
Of obscure dank
Root hollows and
Mist-woven paths,
Pale toadstools and
Dark-reveling worms:
As the skunk walks
By, half vapor, half
Shade, diffusing
The night's uncanny
Essence and atmosphere.

water lily

A hundred
Shallow green
Questions pressed
Upon the
Silent pool,

Before it
Answers all
With a single
Deep white
Syllable.

broom

It starts
Out so well,
Its fresh
Gold straws
Cut square,
Flared wide,

But so often
Ends otherwise,
With weary
Wan bristles
All stubbed
To one side.

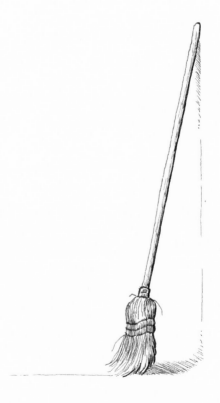

giraffe

How lucky
To live
So high
Above
The body,
Breathing
At heaven's
Level,
Looking
Sun
In the eye;
While down
Below
The neck's
Precarious
Stair,
Back, belly,
And legs
Take care
Of themselves,

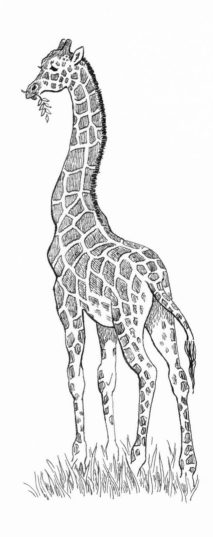

Hardly
Aware
Of the head's
Airy
Affairs.

flies

Flies wear
Their bones
On the outside.

Some show dead
Gray, as bones
Should seem,

But others gleam
Dark blue, or bright
Metal-green,

Or a polished
Copper, mirroring
The sun:

If all bones
Shone so, I
Wouldn't mind

Going around
In my own
Skeleton.